VOCAL SELECTIONS

It Shoulda Been You

BOOK AND LYRICS
BRIAN HARGROVE

MUSIC AND CONCEPT
BARBARA ANSELMI

ADDITIONAL LYRICS BY

JILL ABRAMOVITZ
MICHAEL L. COOPER
CARLA ROSE FISHER
ERNIE LIJOI
WILL RANDALL

Exclusive stock and amateur stage performing rights are represented by
MUSIC THEATRE INTERNATIONAL
421 West 54th Street, New York, New York 10019
Tel. (212) 541-4684
www.mtishows.com
licensing@mtishows.com

ISBN 978-1-4950-5155-5

HAL•LEONARD®
CORPORATION
7777 W. BLUEMOUND RD. P.O. BOX 13819 MILWAUKEE, WI 53213

In Australia Contact:
Hal Leonard Australia Pty. Ltd.
4 Lentara Court
Cheltenham, Victoria, 3192 Australia
Email: ausadmin@halleonard.com.au

Visit Hal Leonard Online at
www.halleonard.com

DARYL ROTH   SCOTT LANDIS
JANE BERGÈRE   JAYNE BARON SHERMAN

PATTY BAKER   BROADWAY ACROSS AMERICA   CLEAR CHANNEL SPECTACOLOR
GLOKEN LLC   JAMES L. NEDERLANDER   JOHN O'BOYLE
JUDITH ANN ABRAMS/JACKI BARLIA FLORIN
OLD CAMPUS PRODUCTIONS/READY TO PLAY
SARA BETH ZIVITZ/PASSERO PRODUCTIONS

PRESENT

TYNE DALY
HARRIET HARRIS
LISA HOWARD   SIERRA BOGGESS

IN

It Shoulda Been You

BOOK AND LYRICS   MUSIC AND CONCEPT
BRIAN HARGROVE   BARBARA ANSELMI

WITH

DAVID BURTKA   MONTEGO GLOVER   CHIP ZIEN
JOSH GRISETTI

ADAM HELLER   MICHAEL X. MARTIN
ANNE L. NATHAN   NICK SPANGLER

FARAH ALVIN   GINA FERRALL   AARON C. FINLEY   MITCH GREENBERG   JILLIAN LOUIS

AND

EDWARD HIBBERT

SCENIC DESIGN	COSTUME DESIGN	LIGHTING DESIGN	SOUND DESIGN
ANNA LOUIZOS	WILLIAM IVEY LONG	KEN BILLINGTON	NEVIN STEINBERG

HAIR DESIGN	MAKE-UP DESIGN	ASSOCIATE DIRECTOR	ASSOCIATE CHOREOGRAPHER
PAUL HUNTLEY	ANNE FORD-COATES	SHELLEY BUTLER	LEE A. WILKINS

ORCHESTRATOR	ORCHESTRA COORDINATOR	CASTING	PRODUCTION STAGE MANAGER
DOUG BESTERMAN	JOHN MILLER	JAY BINDER, CSA, TARA RUBIN, CSA & MERRI SUGARMAN, CSA	BESS MARIE GLORIOSO

TECHNICAL SUPERVISION	PRESS REPRESENTATIVE	MARKETING	GENERAL MANAGEMENT
JUNIPER STREET PRODUCTIONS	O&M CO.	TYPE A MARKETING	FORESIGHT THEATRICAL ALLAN WILLIAMS

MUSIC DIRECTION AND ARRANGEMENTS
LAWRENCE YURMAN

CHOREOGRAPHED BY
JOSH RHODES

DIRECTED BY
DAVID HYDE PIERCE

World Premiere production produced by George Street Playhouse September 2011 – David Saint, Artistic Director
and was Further Developed and Produced by Village Theatre, Issaquah, Washington
Robb Hunt, Executive Producer – Steve Tomkins, Artistic Director
It Shoulda Been You was presented at the National Alliance for Musical Theatre's Festival of New Musicals in 2009. www.namt.org
The Producers wish to express their appreciation to the Theatre Development Fund for its support of this production.

I NEVER WANTED THIS

Words by BRIAN HARGROVE and MICHAEL COOPER
Music by BARBARA ANSELMI

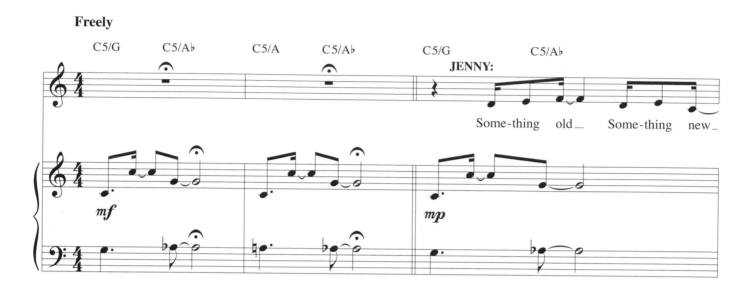

Moderately, but with intensity (♩ = 114)

Day…"   On this

day of cel - e - bra - tion   Where you've   bare - ly slept _ a   wink, _   Oh this

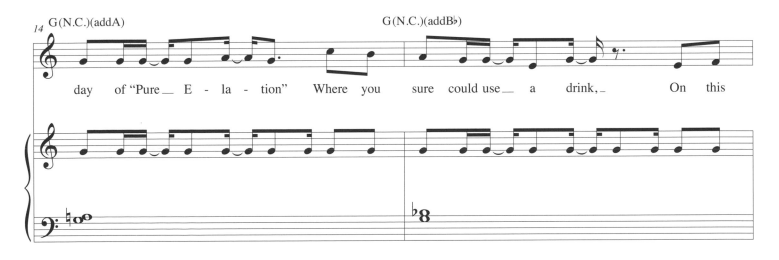

day   of "Pure _ E - la - tion"   Where you   sure could use _ a   drink, _   On this

day   of ag - gra - va - tion   When you   think: I nev - er

PERFECT

Words by BRIAN HARGROVE and CARLA ROSE FISHER
Music by BARBARA ANSELMI

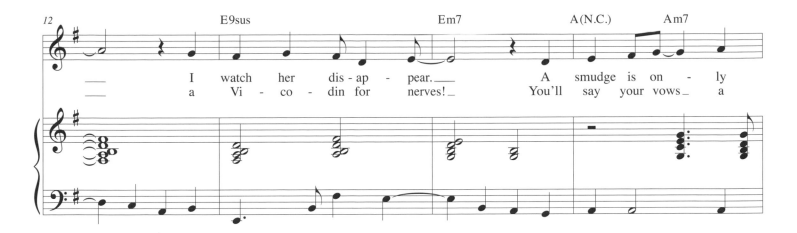

I watch her dis - ap - pear.___ A smudge is on - ly
___ a Vi - co - din for nerves!___ You'll say your vows___ a

trag - ic if it shows.___ You're gon - na be per - fect.___
few feet off the floor!___ It's gon na be per - fect.___

All you have to do___ is smile.___ And it's my job___ to get___
Not one place card out___ of place.___ I'll han - dle Mom's___ neu - ro -

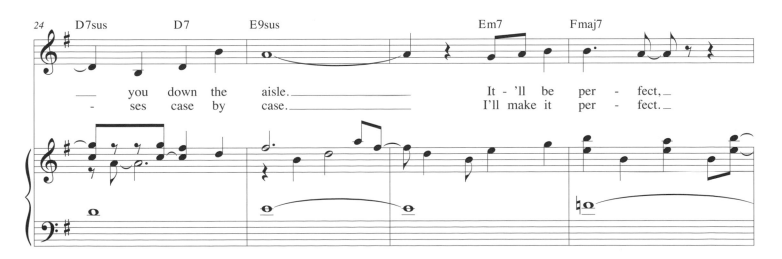

___ you down the aisle.___ It - 'll be per - fect,___
- ses case by case.___ I'll make it per - fect.___

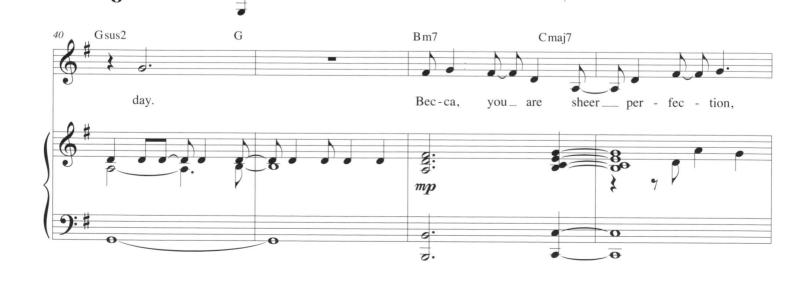

you don't have to try.___ You're ev-'ry-thing Mom want-ed me to

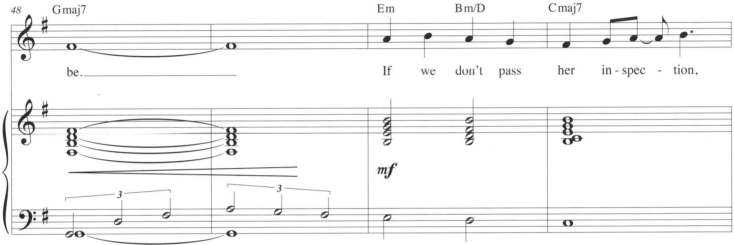

be._____ If we don't pass her in-spec-tion,

No one's gon-na die.___ She'll on-ly spend a life-time blam-ing me!___

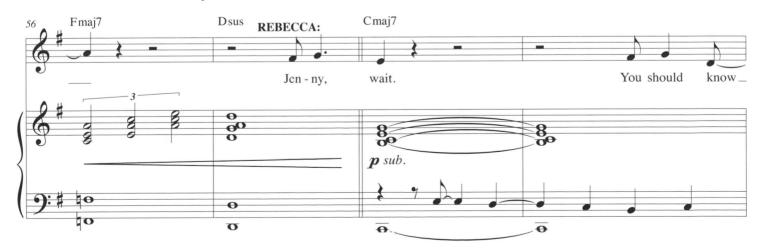

REBECCA:

Jen-ny, wait. You should know___

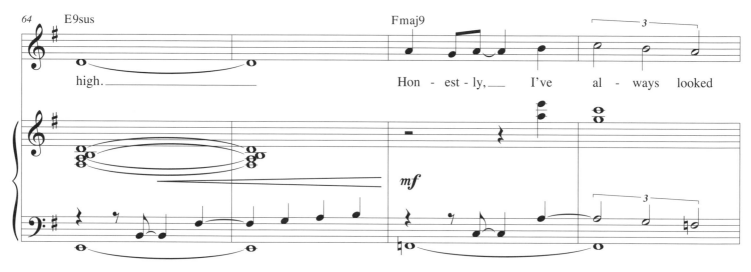

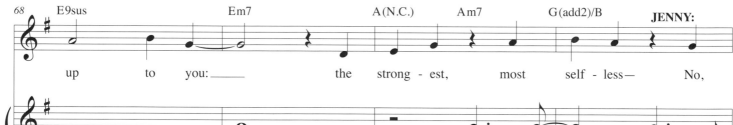

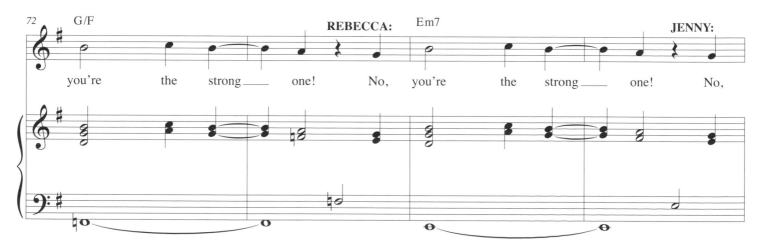

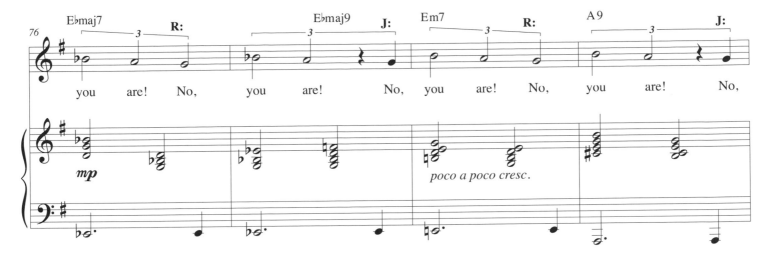

you are! No, you are! No, you are! No, you are! No,

you! No, you! No, you! No, you! No, you! It's _____ got-ta be

per - fect! _____ We can be

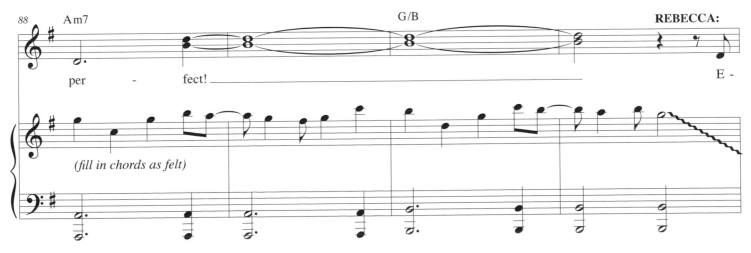

per - fect! _____ E-

IT SHOULDA BEEN YOU

Words by BRIAN HARGROVE and WILL RANDALL
Music by BARBARA ANSELMI

knows you nev-er mar-ry when you're in your goy-im phase. He's so white bread, he sweats

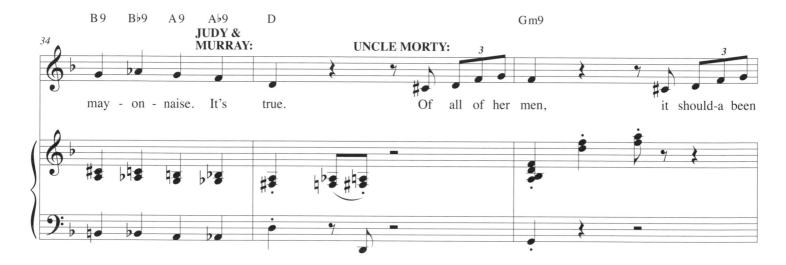

may-on-naise. It's true. Of all of her men, it should-a been

you. Who are you a-gain? It's not too

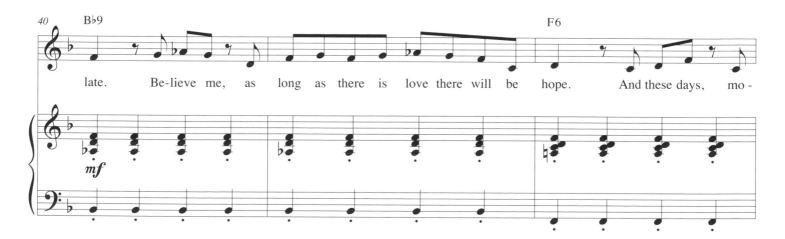

late. Be-lieve me, as long as there is love there will be hope. And these days, mo-

WHO

Words by BRIAN HARGROVE
Music by BARBARA ANSELMI

Who got you in-to Yale? Who? Who's known you bet-ter than

an - y - one,_____ since you were e - lev - en?

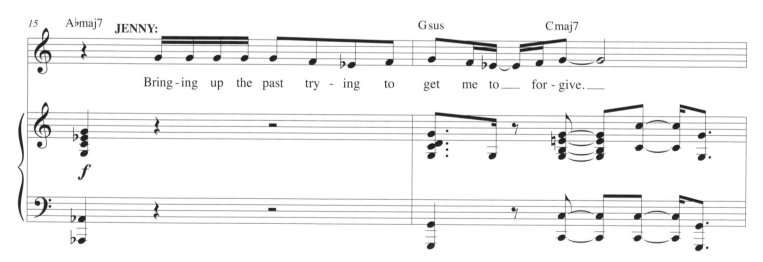

JENNY:

Bring-ing up the past try - ing to get me to____ for - give.____

Hop - ing I might let you off the hook.

Jen - ny, think back. We were once_ best friends. We used_ to

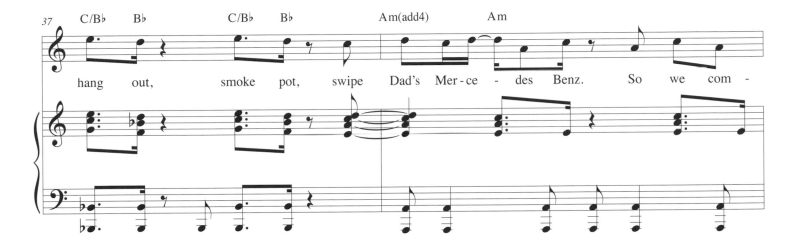

hang out, smoke pot, swipe Dad's Mer - ce - des Benz. So we com -

mit - ted crimes._____ Man, they were

such good_ times!_

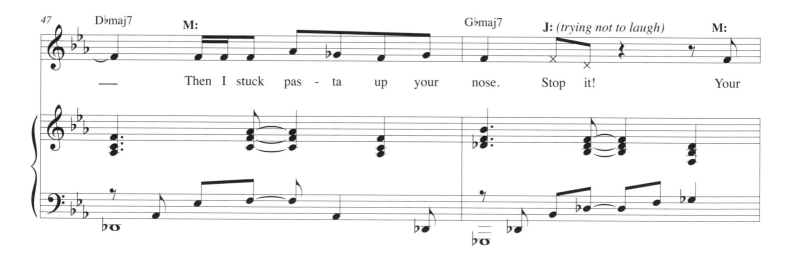

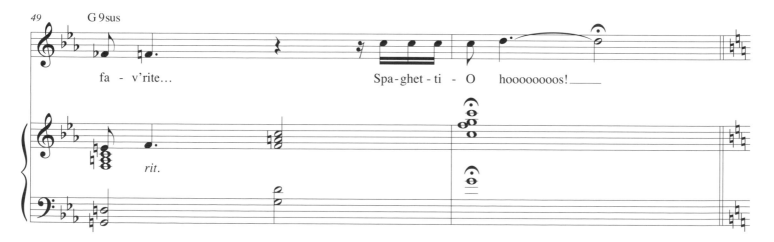

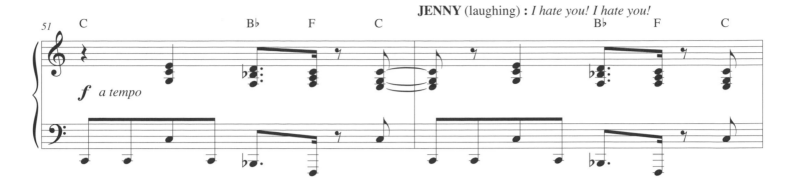

JENNY (laughing) : *I hate you! I hate you!*

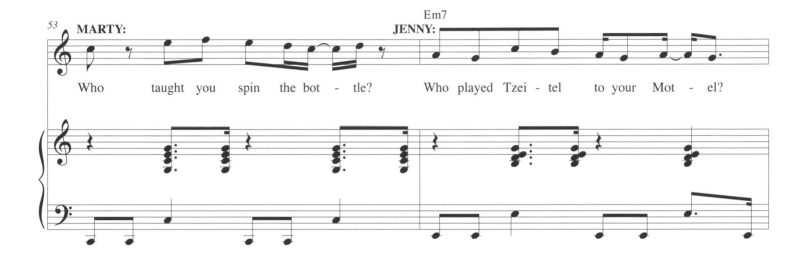

MARTY: Who taught you spin the bot-tle? JENNY: Who played Tzei-tel to your Mot-el?

MARTY: Who cheers you up when you're blue?___ Come on say___ it!

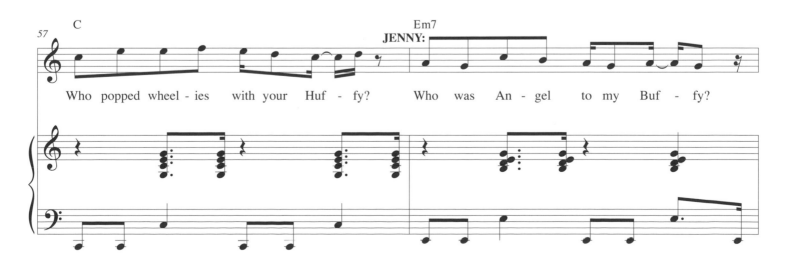

JENNY: Who popped wheel-ies with your Huf-fy? Who was An-gel to my Buf-fy?

Who's the big - gest nut you ev - er knew?   It's

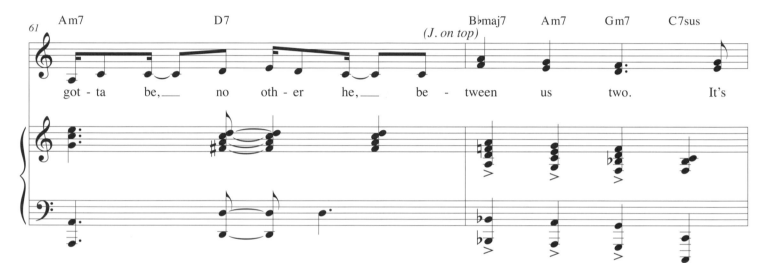

got - ta be,___ no oth - er he,___ be - tween us two.   It's

you know, you *know* you know._____

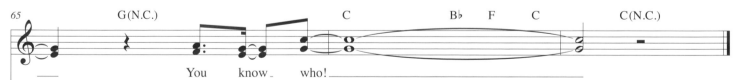

You know___ who!_____

BACK IN THE DAY

Words by BRIAN HARGROVE
Music by BARBARA ANSELMI

Light Swing, feels like it's in 2 (♩ = 115)

GEORGE:

Back in the day, my dad was not my friend. We were like

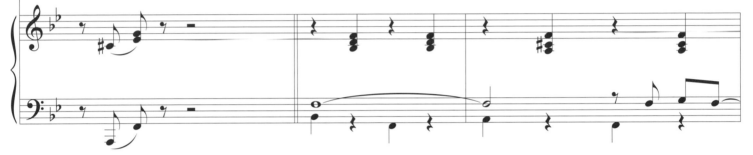

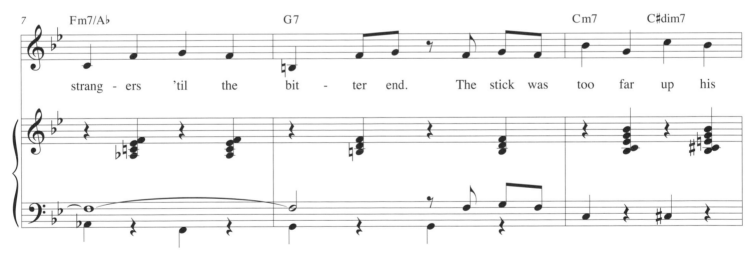

strang- ers 'til the bit - ter end. The stick was too far up his

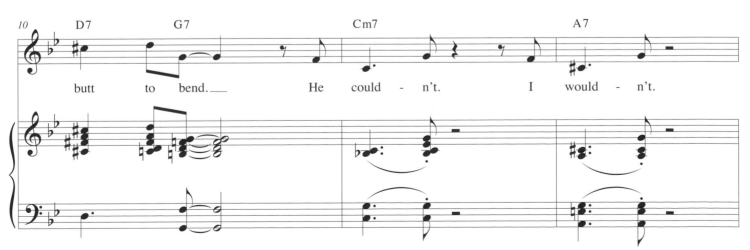

butt to bend.___ He could - n't. I would - n't.

GEORGE: *Walk with me, son...*

Back in the day, the soft stuff went un-said. To say, "I love you," filled a man with dread. My fa-ther

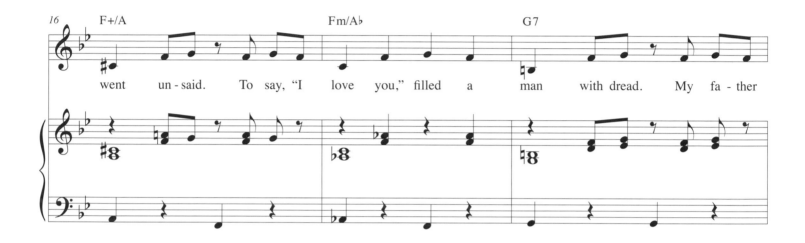

said it once and then dropped dead.__ You can't have feel-ings when you wear the

pants. Come on let's dance.__

GEORGE:

Back in the day, a man knew where he stood. He wed a

girl from his own neigh-bor-hood. She gave her word, you knew that word was good. But

now a girl's pri-or-i-ties can shift... You get my drift?!

(GEORGE scats)

Shuf-fle ball change.

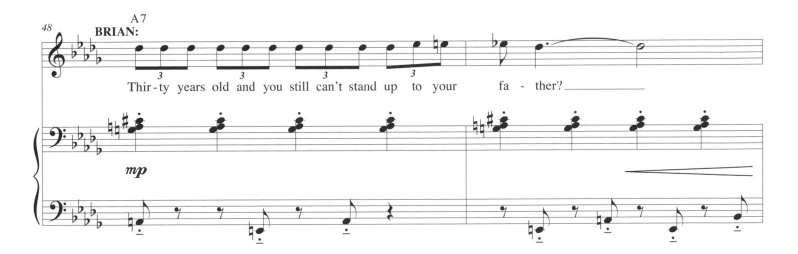

Thir-ty years old and you still can't stand up to your fa - ther?

Dec-ades of si - lence, still you've got noth-ing to say?

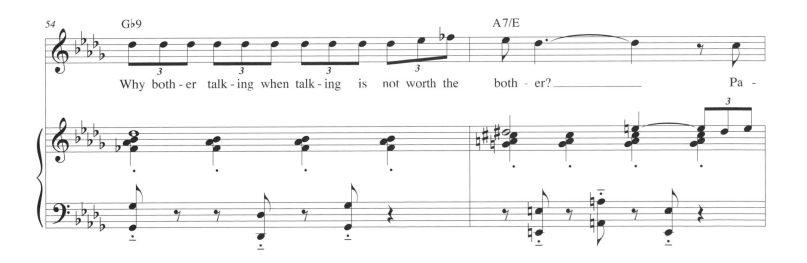

Why both-er talk-ing when talk-ing is not worth the both - er? Pa -

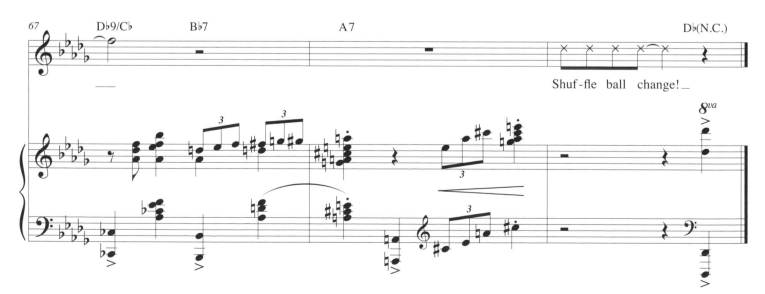

NICE

Words by BRIAN HARGROVE
Music by BARBARA ANSELMI

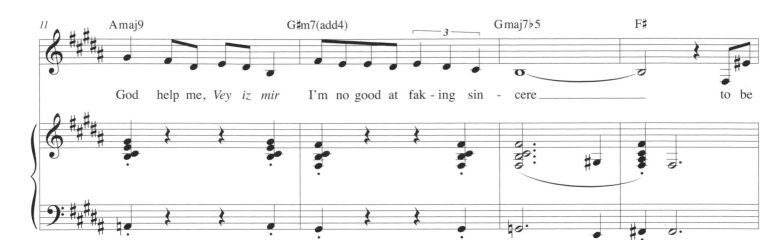

God help me, *Vey iz mir* I'm no good at fak-ing sin - cere_____ to be

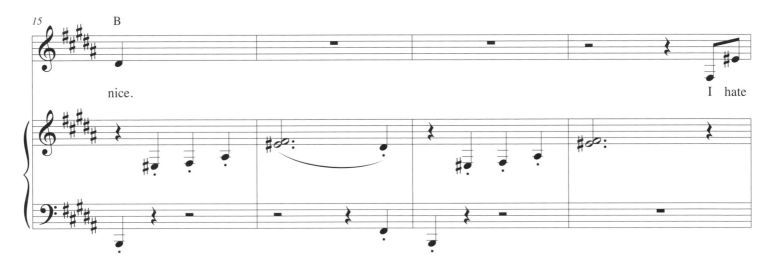

nice. I hate

nice. Nice is lies. It's be-friend - ing a bitch you de-

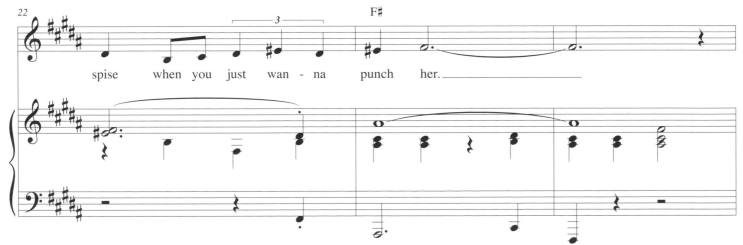

spise when you just wan - na punch her._____

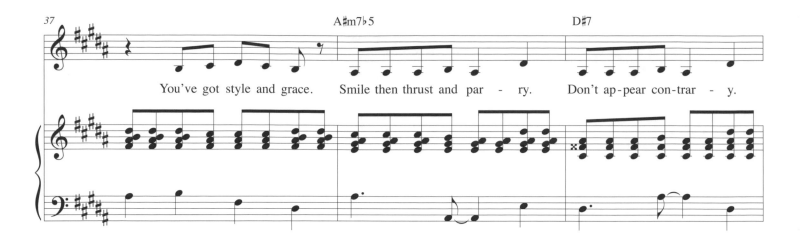

You've got style and grace. Smile then thrust and par - ry. Don't ap-pear con-trar - y.

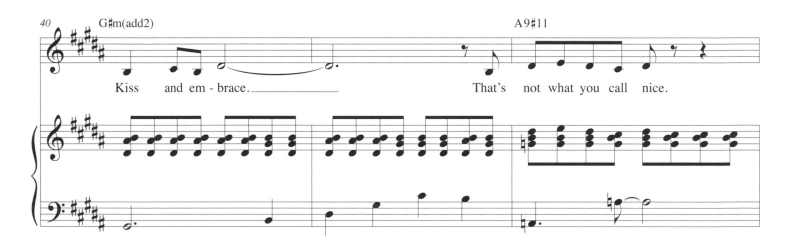

Kiss and em - brace._____ That's not what you call nice.

It's ba - lo-ney. The nice you know is real, not pho - ny. For

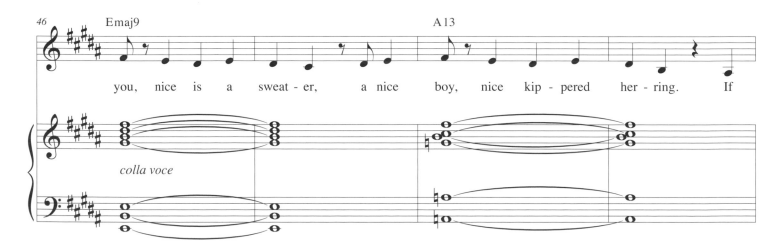

you, nice is a sweat - er, a nice boy, nice kip - pered her - ring. If

Tempo I

you don't speak up soon you could start swear-ing.

I like

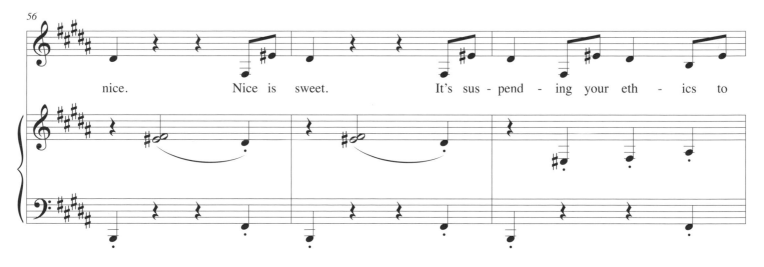

nice.   Nice is sweet.   It's sus-pend - ing your eth - ics to

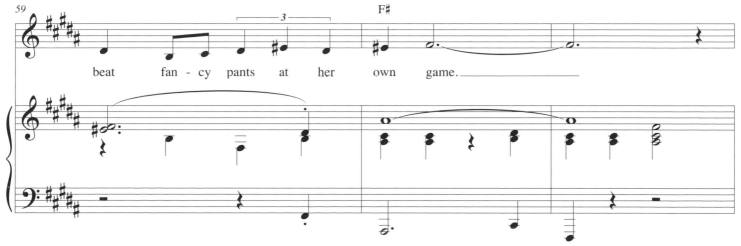

beat   fan - cy pants at   her   own   game.

Oy boy, am I *fer-klempt.* It's bet-ter then I ev-er dreamt.

Play-ing nice.

Here's to nice! Nice is grand! It's ex-

tend-ing a wel-com-ing hand while you smack with the oth-er.

WHERE DID I GO WRONG

Words by BRIAN HARGROVE
Music by BARBARA ANSELMI

*Sung an octave lower in the Broadway production

BEAUTIFUL

Words by BRIAN HARGROVE and ERNIE LIJOI
Music by BARBARA ANSELMI

54

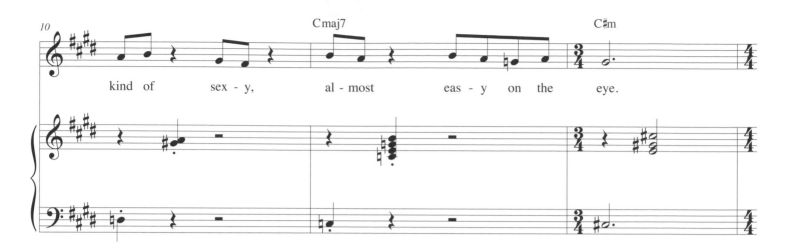

kind of sex - y, al - most eas - y on the eye.

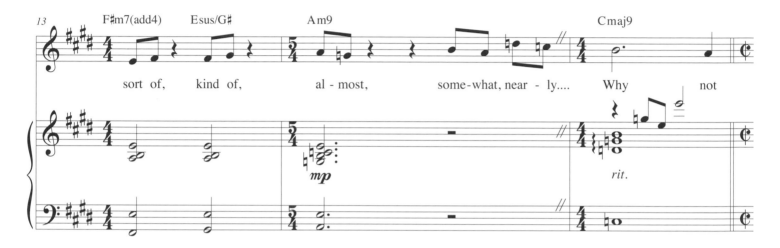

sort of, kind of, al - most, some-what, near - ly.... Why not

Lightly, in 2

beau - ti - ful?_____ I am kind, al - ways kind.

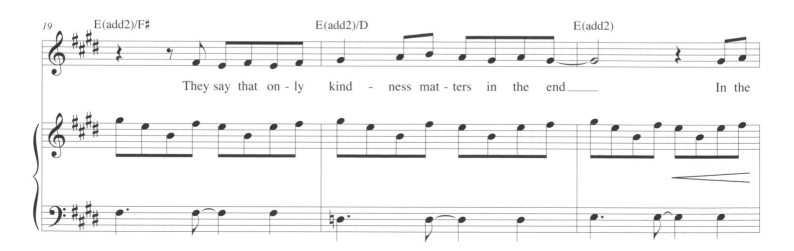

They say that on - ly kind - ness mat - ters in the end_____ In the

LOVE YOU TILL THE DAY

Words by BRAIN HARGROVE and ERNIE LIJOI
Music by BARBARA ANSELMI

Heart-felt, '80s Ballad style

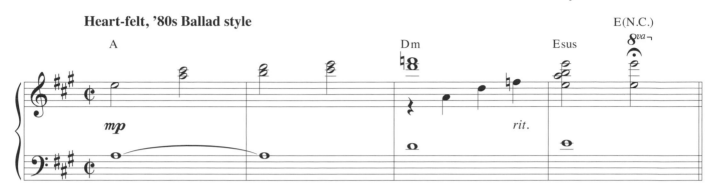

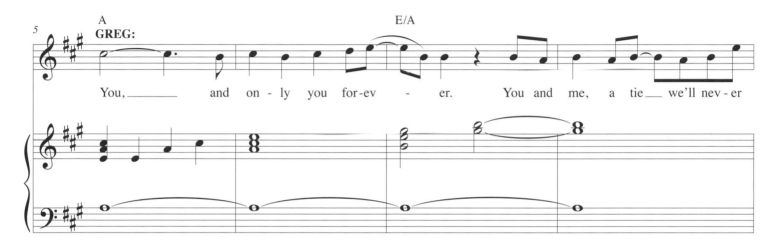

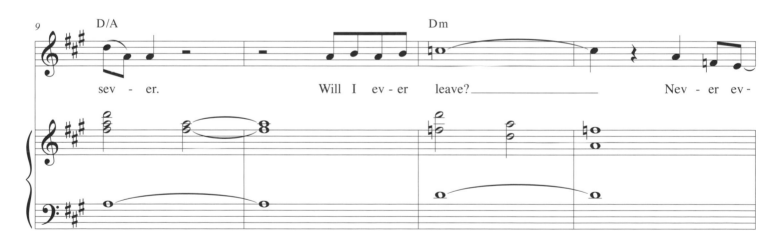

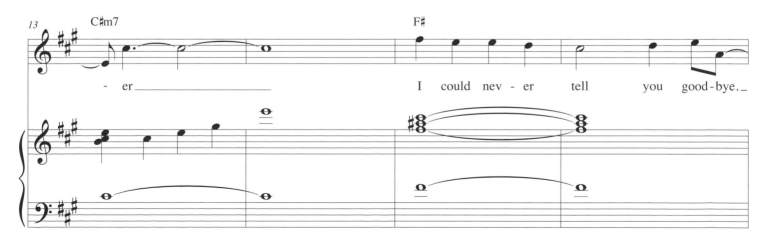

I'll love you till the day ___ you die ___

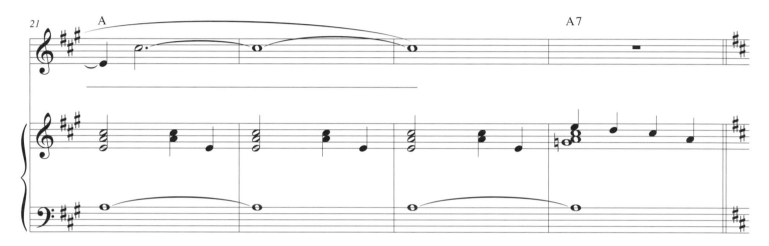

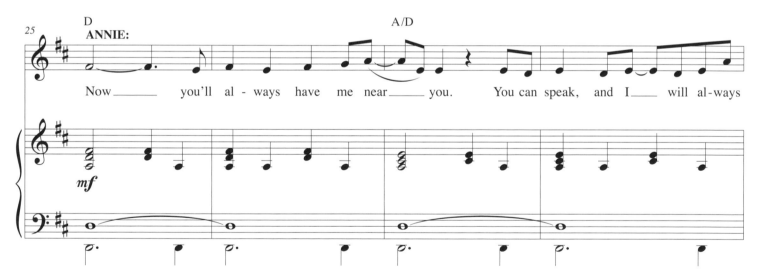

ANNIE:
Now ___ you'll al-ways have me near ___ you. You can speak, and I ___ will al-ways

hear ___ you. Want to know the truth? ___ I re - vere ___

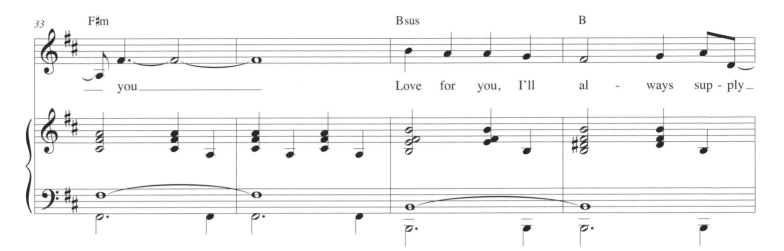

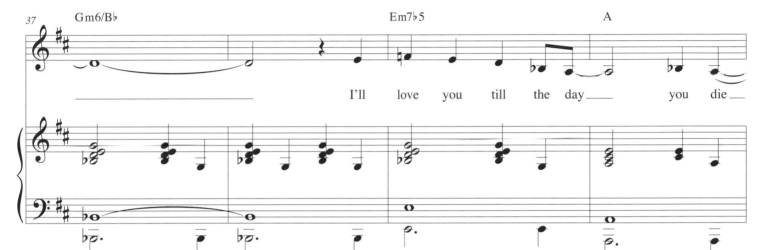

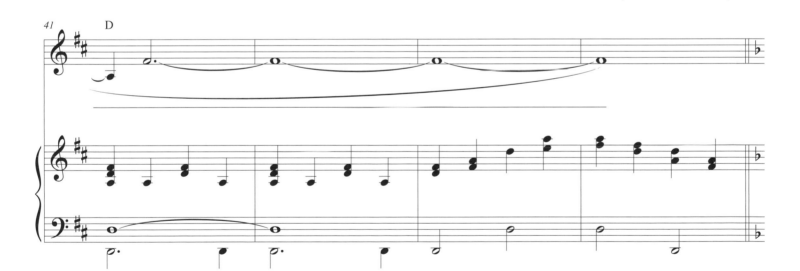

did. And I did be-cause_ I love you more than life it-self

GREG: Not be-cause you're hav-ing my kid

ANNIE: Ah!_

Ah!_

Till the ea-gles

For- ev - er..._

JENNY'S BLUES

Words by BRIAN HARGROVE
Music by BARBARA ANSELMI

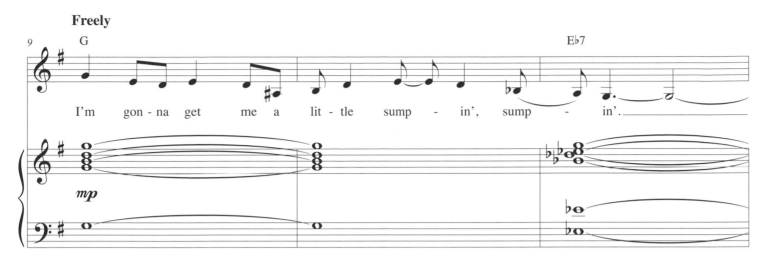

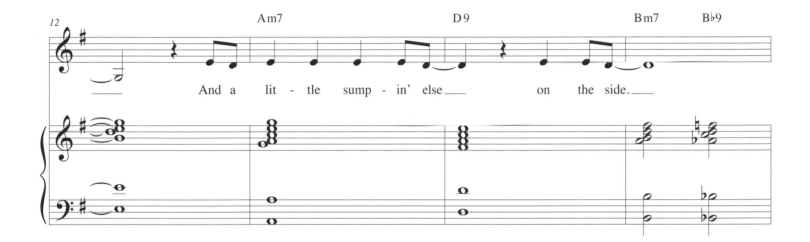

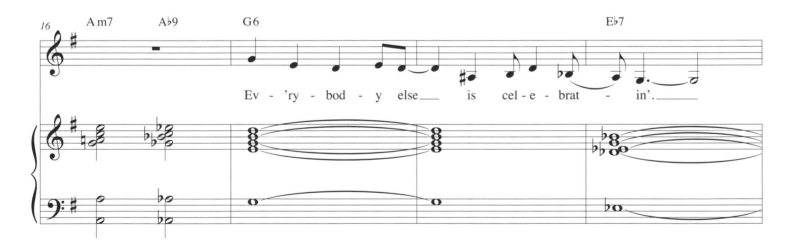

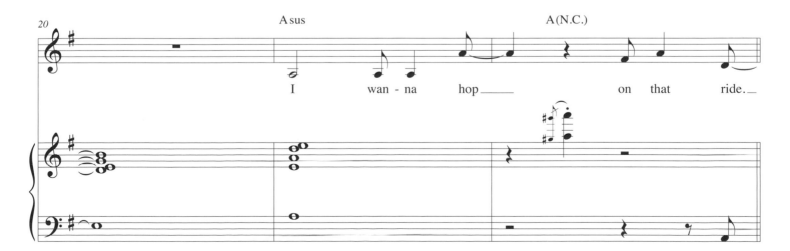

Lazy Swing ($\textstyle\quad$ = 116)

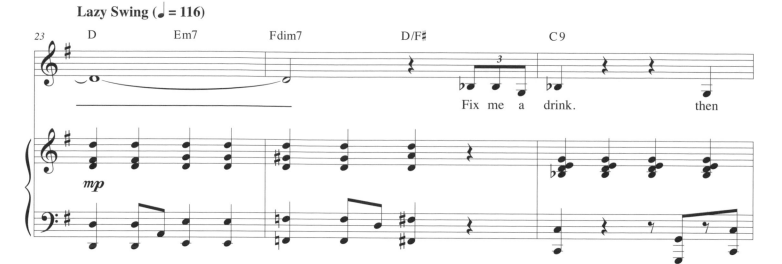

Fix me a drink. then

dou - ble it up.___ And when my glass is emp - ty, re - fill my cup.___

___ 'Cause I'm gon - na get me a lit - tle sump - in', sump -

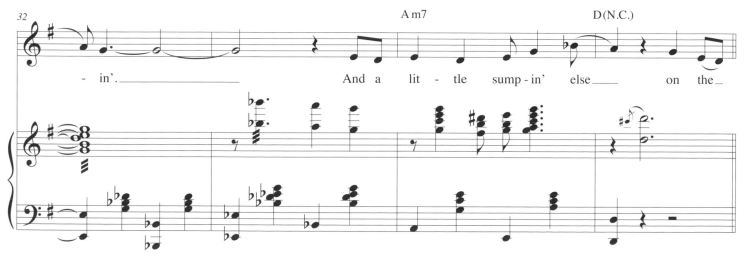

- in'._____ And a lit - tle sump - in' else___ on the___

Slightly slower and building

I've spent my whole damn life ___ just wait - in'. ___

Oth - ers danced while I just sat ___ on the shelf. ___

I have lived to

please, ain't no ___ de - bat - in'. ___

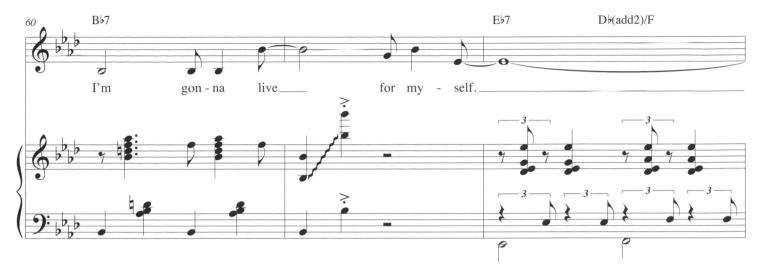

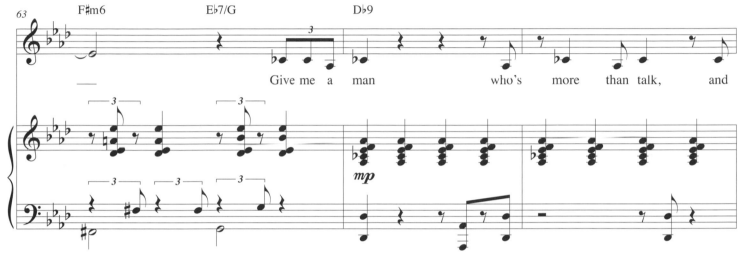

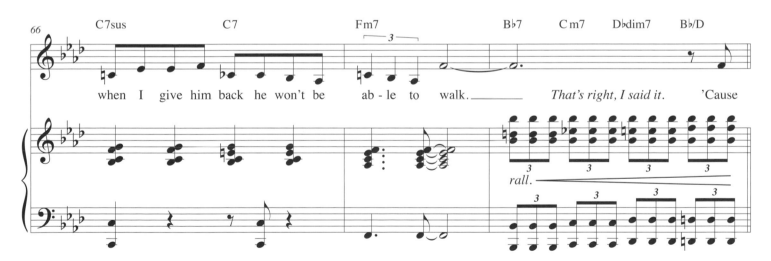

Cakewalk

WHATEVER

Words by BRIAN HARGROVE
Music by BARBARA ANSELMI

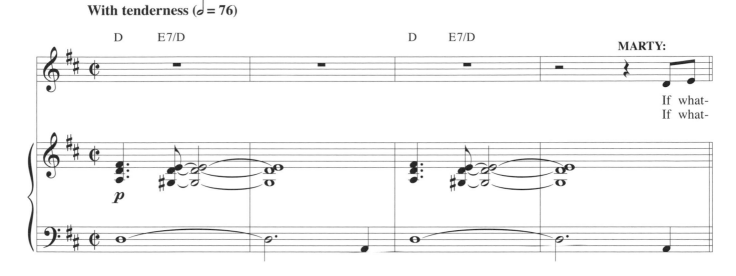

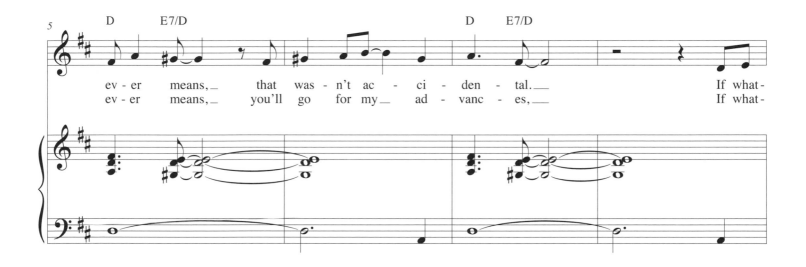

ev-er means,___ you need me to___ be gen - tle_____ } Then
ev-er means,___ we both get sec - ond chanc - es_____

I'll take___ what-ev - er, when-ev - er._____

I'll take___ what-ev - er, when-ev - er.___

You don't have to know___ That I___ have al - ways felt this way.___

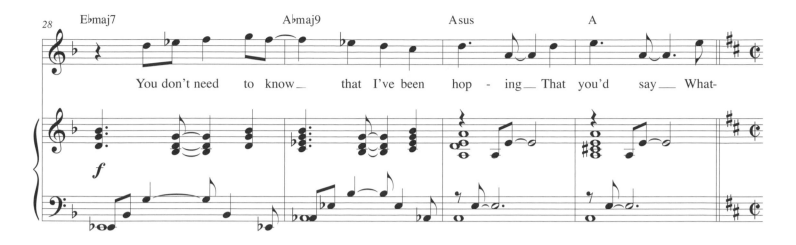

You don't need to know__ that I've been hop - ing__ That you'd say__ What-

Tempo I

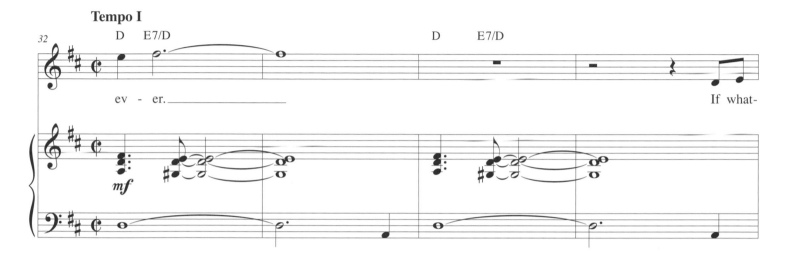

ev - er.____ If what-

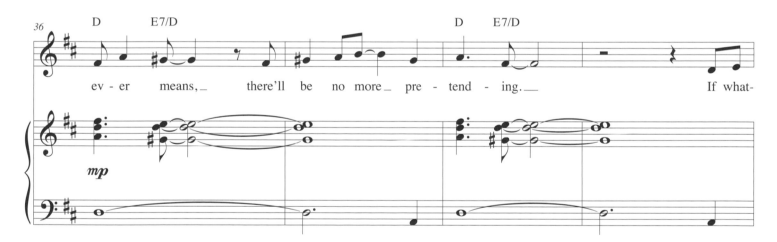

ev - er means,__ there'll be no more__ pre - tend - ing.__ If what-

ev - er means,__ you feel the same__ way too.__ If what-

76

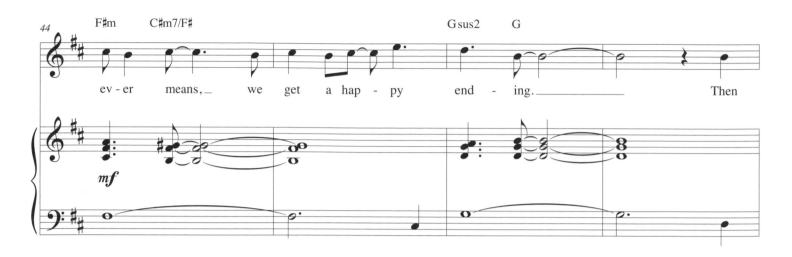

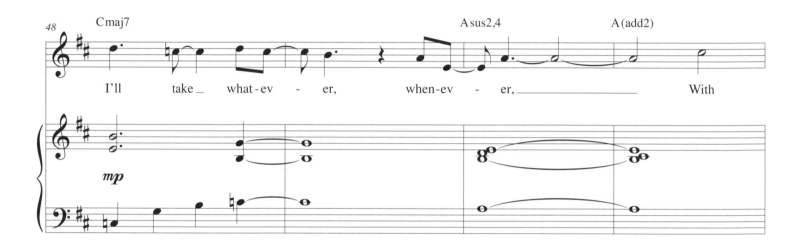

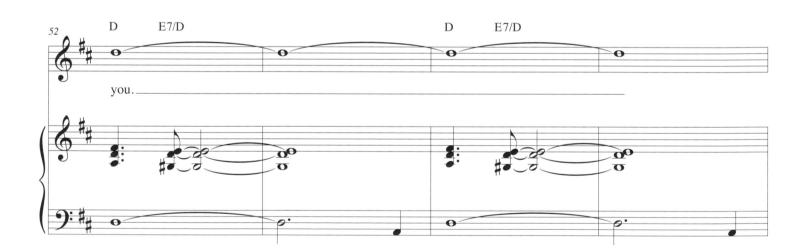

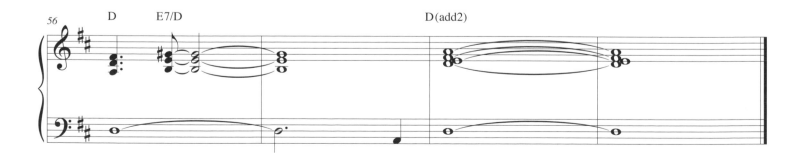

A LITTLE BIT LESS THAN

Words by BRIAN HARGROVE
Music by BARBARA ANSELMI

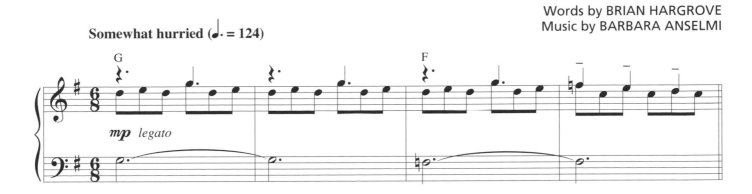

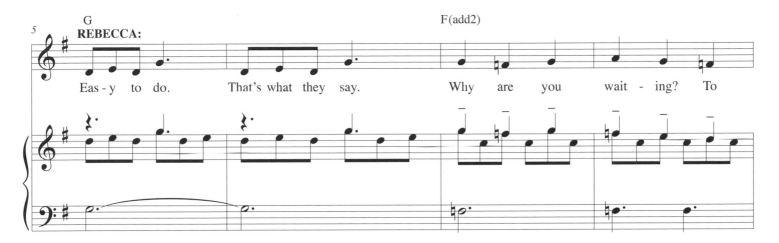

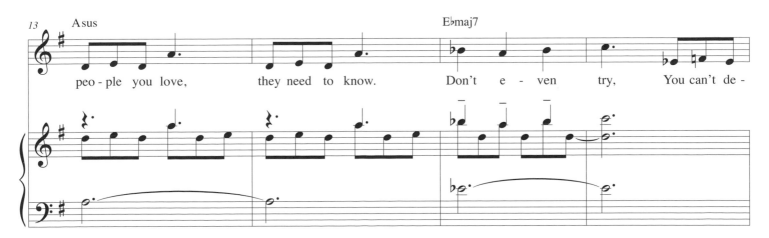

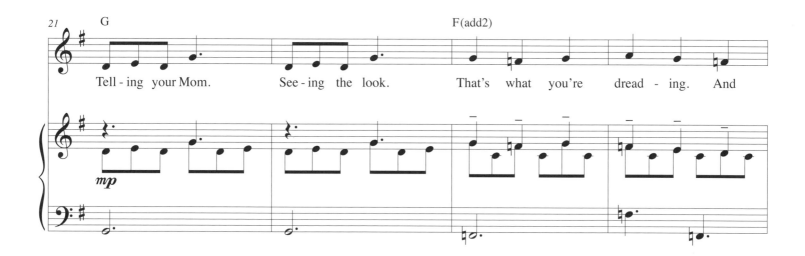

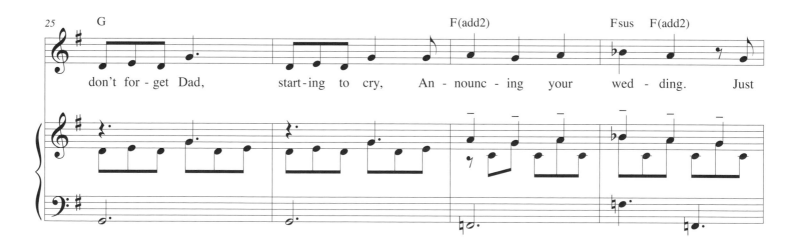

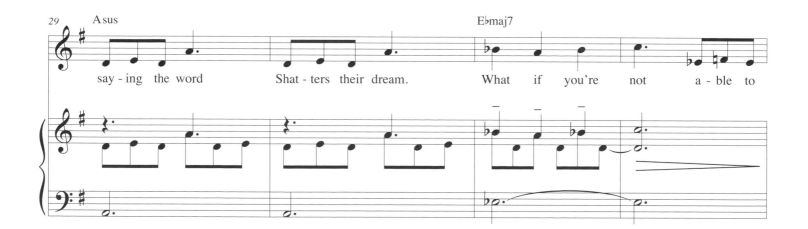

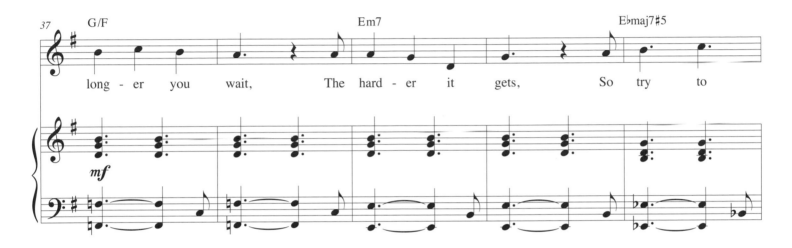

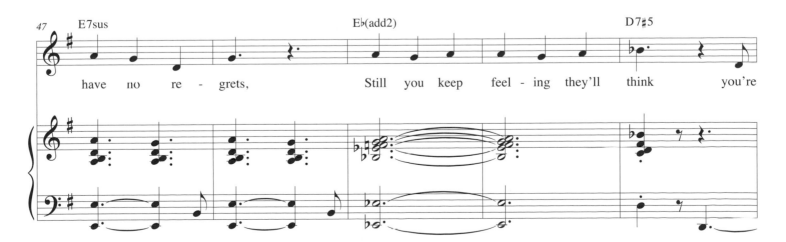

end it._____ And the

long - er you wait, The hard - er it gets, So

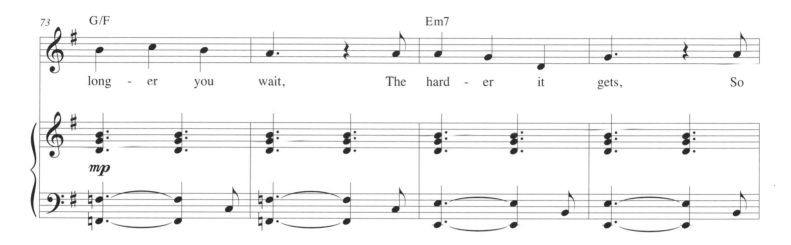

bet - ter stick to the plan._____ Be

true to your - self, you'll have no re - grets,

82

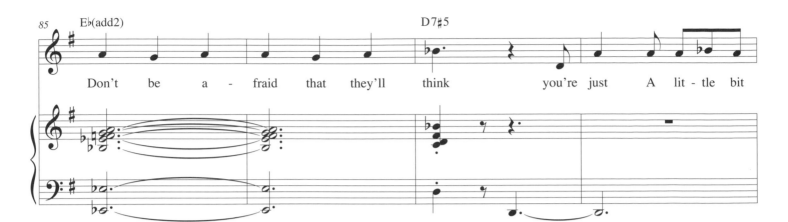

Don't be a - fraid that they'll think you're just A lit - tle bit

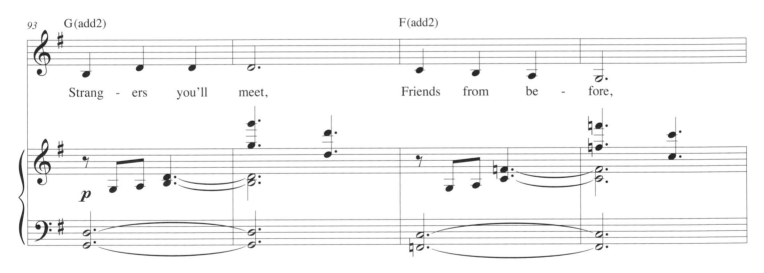

less than.

Strang - ers you'll meet, Friends from be - fore,

Step to the edge, Walk through the door.

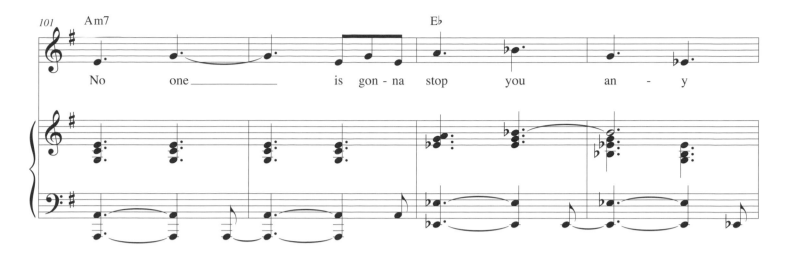

No one_____ is gon-na stop you an - y

more._____

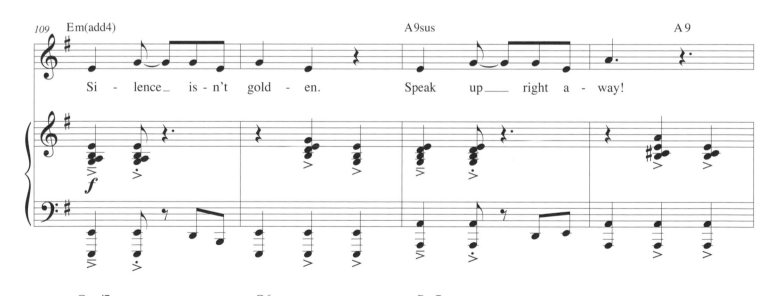

Si - lence__ is-n't gold - en. Speak up__ right a - way!

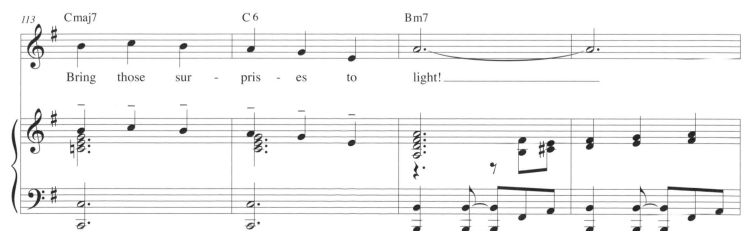

Bring those sur - pris - es to light!_____

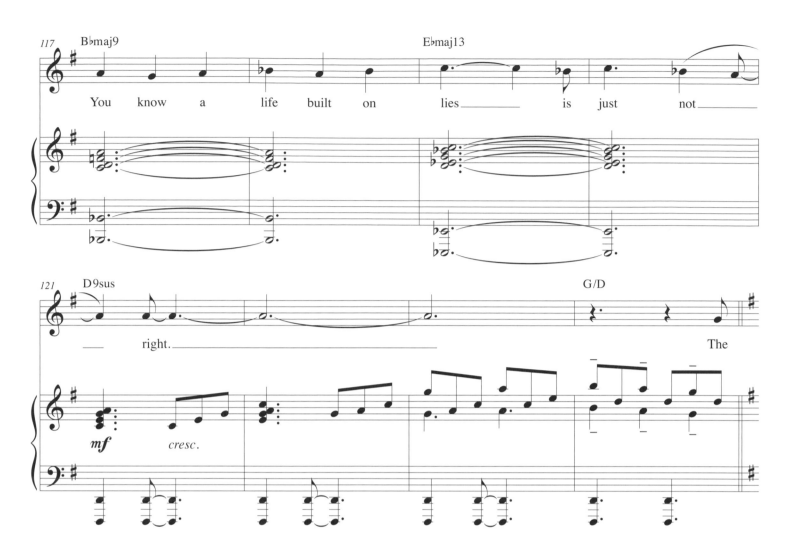

You know a life built on lies_____ is just not_____ right._____ The

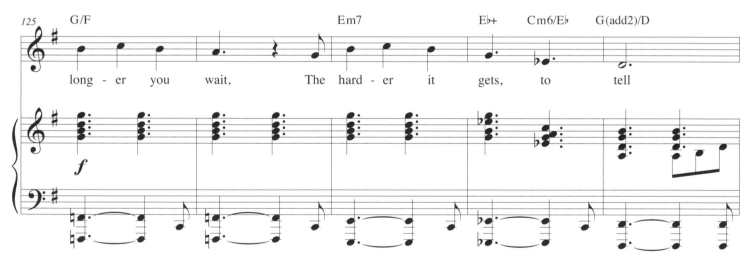

long - er you wait, The hard - er it gets, to tell them._____ The more you pre - tend, The

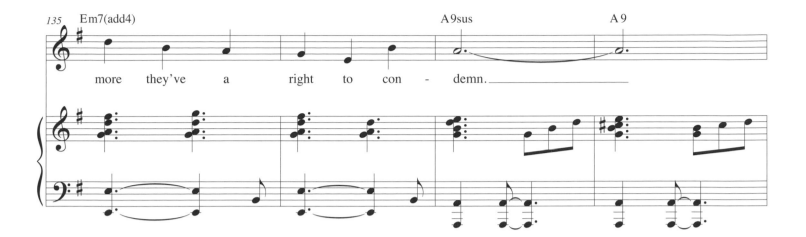

more they've a right to con - demn._____

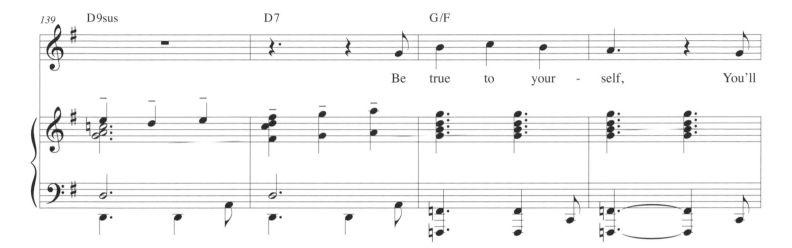

Be true to your - self, You'll

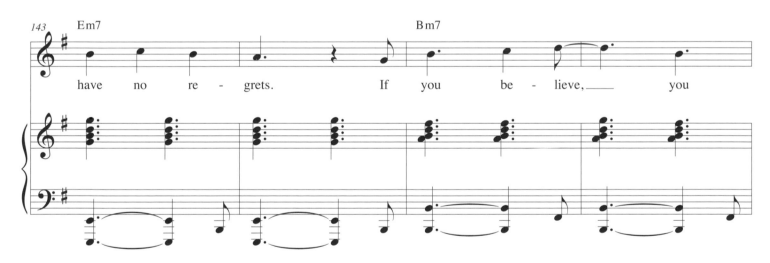

have no re - grets. If you be - lieve,_____ you

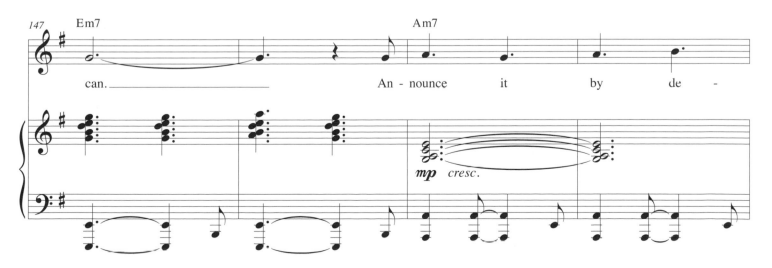

can._____ An - nounce it by de -

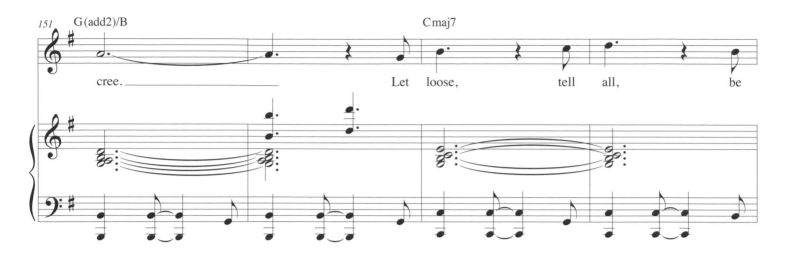

cree._____ Let loose, tell all, be

free!_____ If I

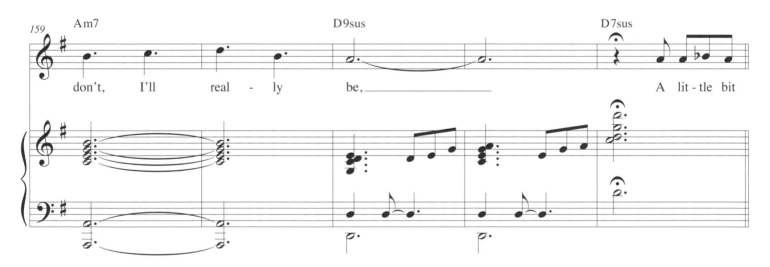

don't, I'll real - ly be,_____ A lit - tle bit

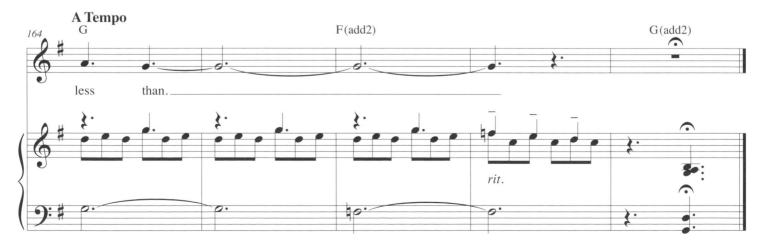

less than._____

WHAT THEY NEVER TELL YOU

Words by BRIAN HARGROVE and JILL ABRAMOVITZ
Music by BARBARA ANSELMI

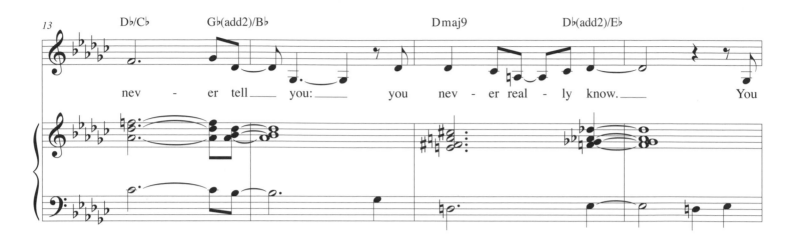

nev - er tell___ you:___ you nev - er real - ly know.___ You

get a feel - ing, feel a some-thing, take a breath__ and go.___ There's

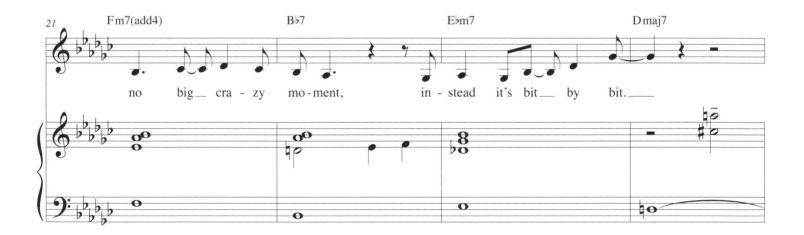

no big__ cra - zy mo - ment, in - stead it's bit__ by bit.___

You'll make him laugh, he'll make you soup, the

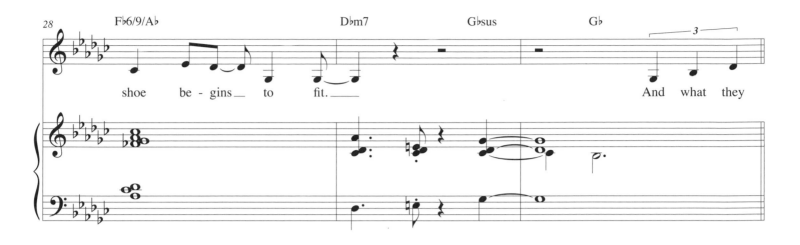

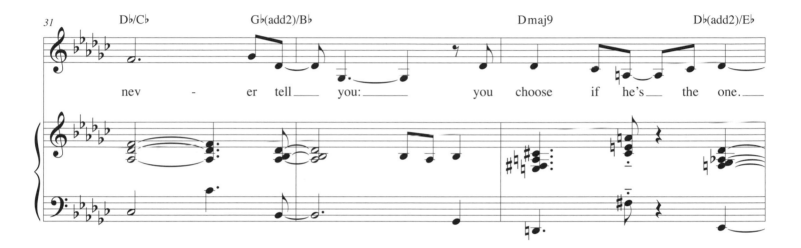

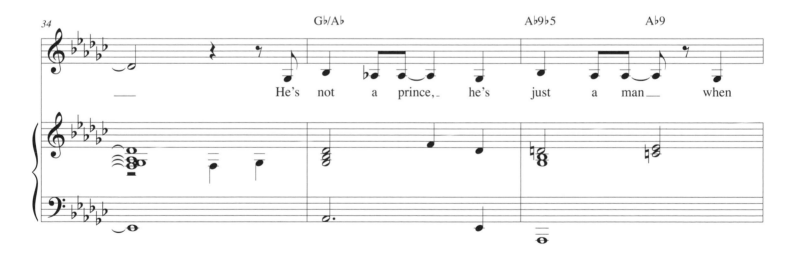

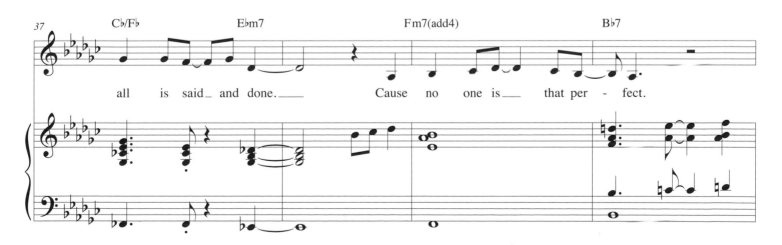

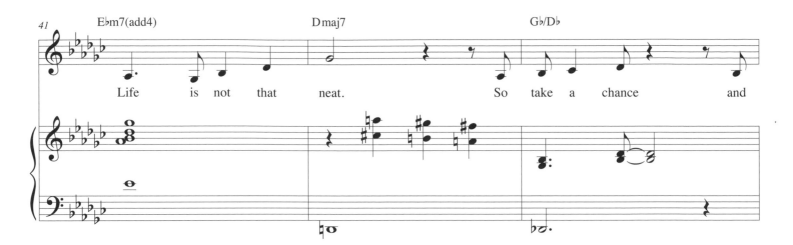

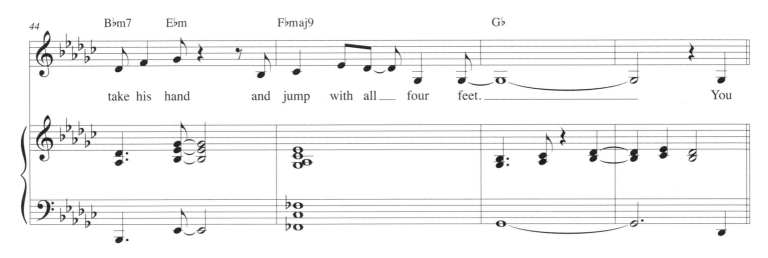

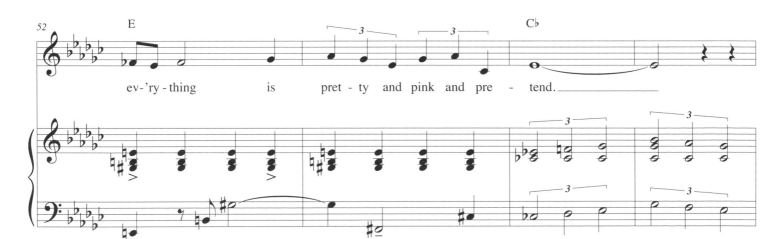

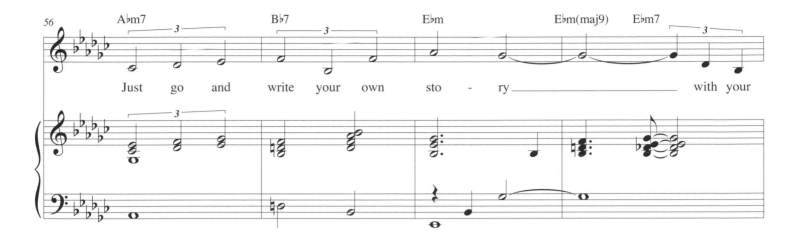

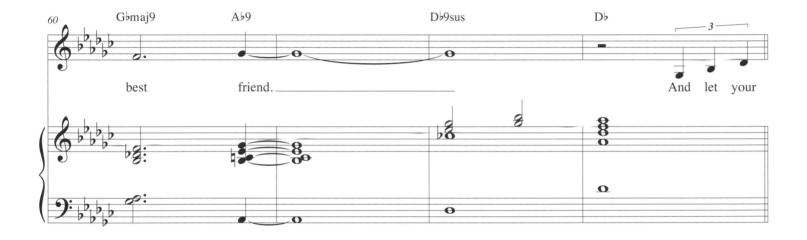

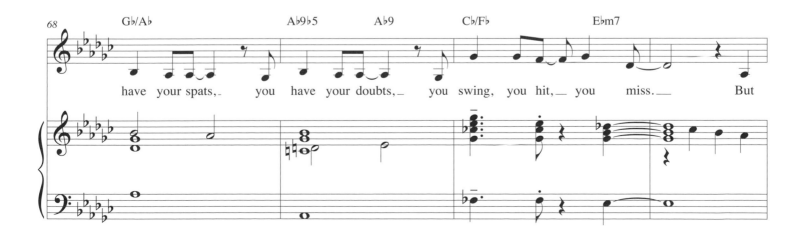

ask me if ___ it's worth ___ it, would I do it all a -

Freely

gain? _____ When I sit with my girls ___ and I *kvell* from my life ___ and I

colla voce   *rit.*

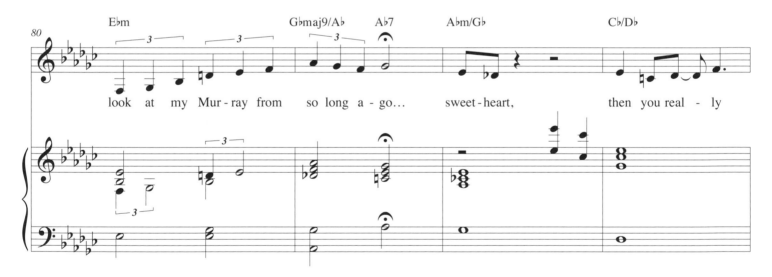

look at my Mur - ray from so long a - go... sweet - heart, then you real - ly

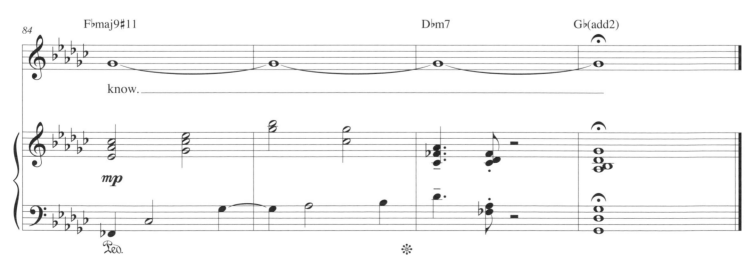

know. _____

THAT'S FAMILY

Words by BRIAN HARGROVE
Music by BARBARA ANSELMI

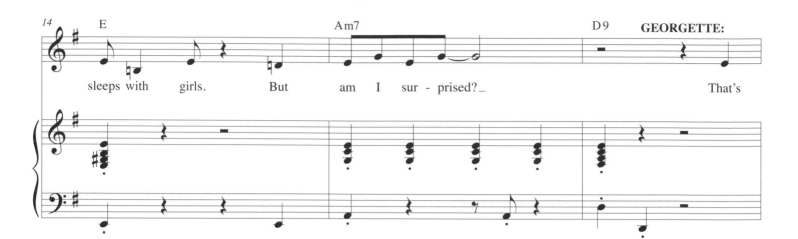

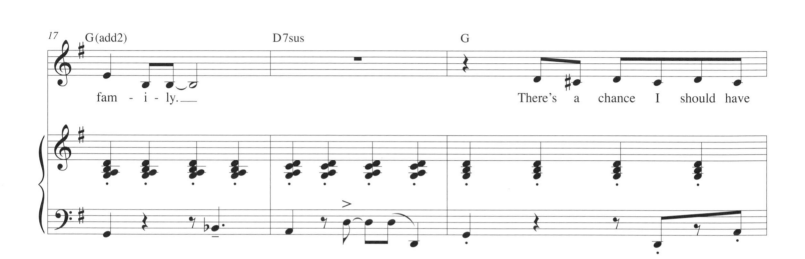

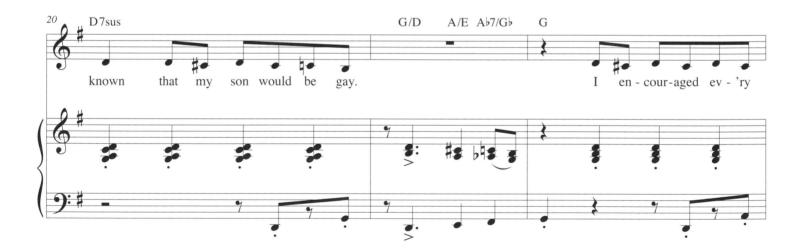

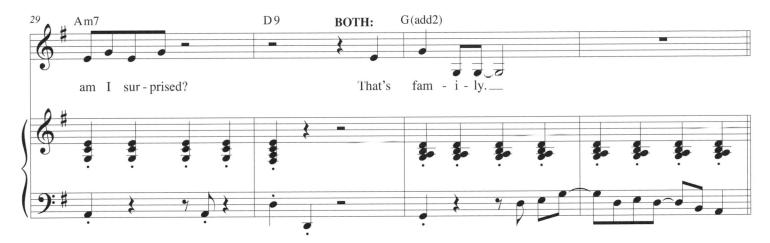

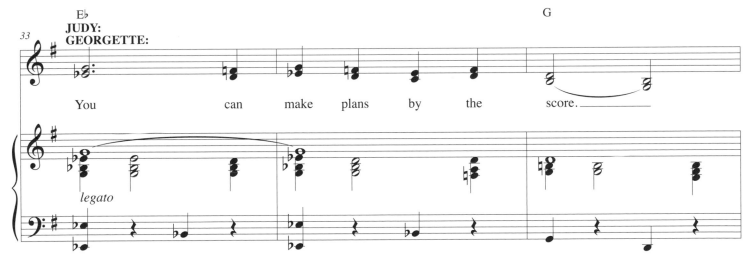

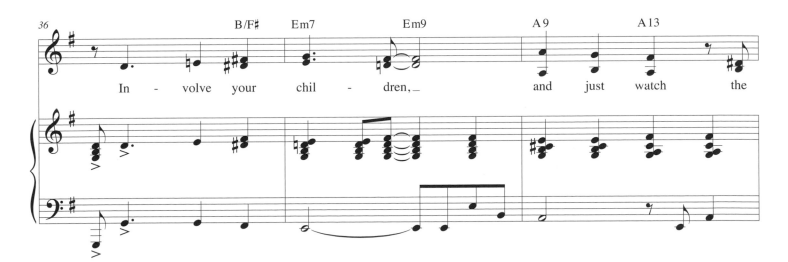

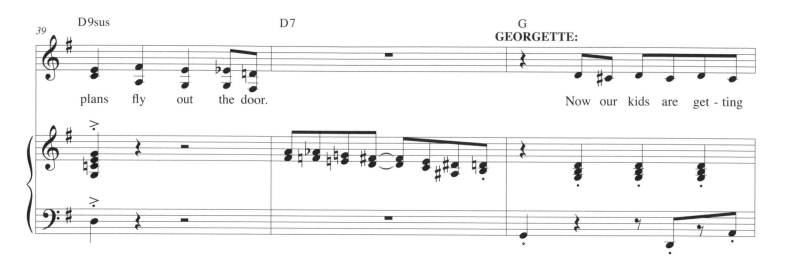

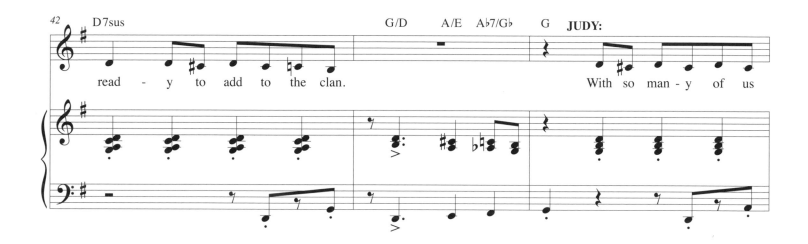

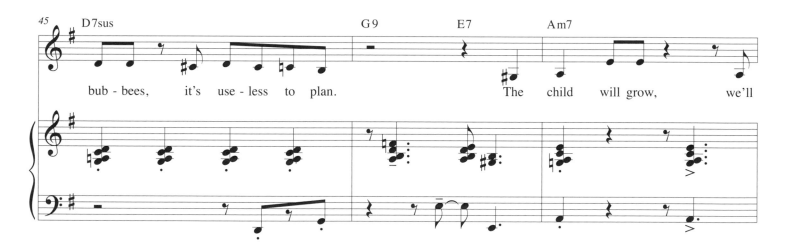

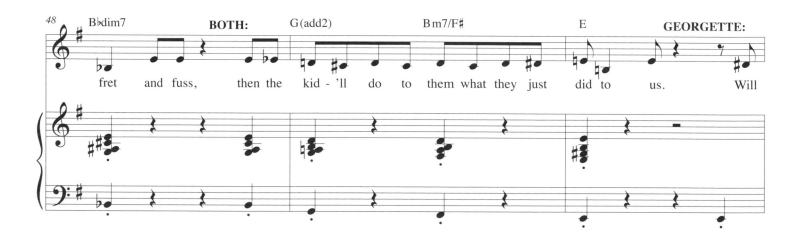

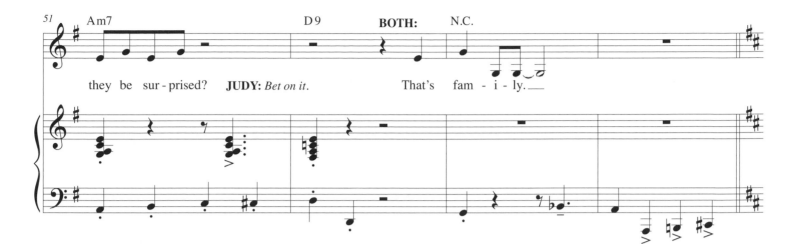

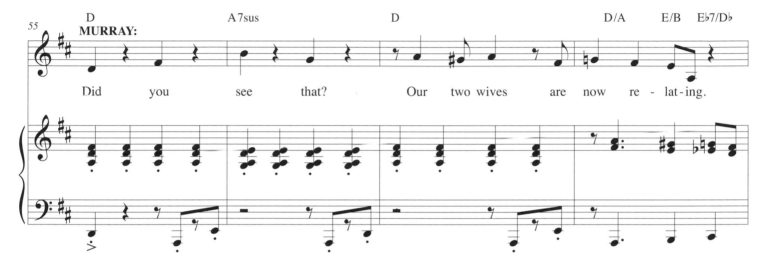

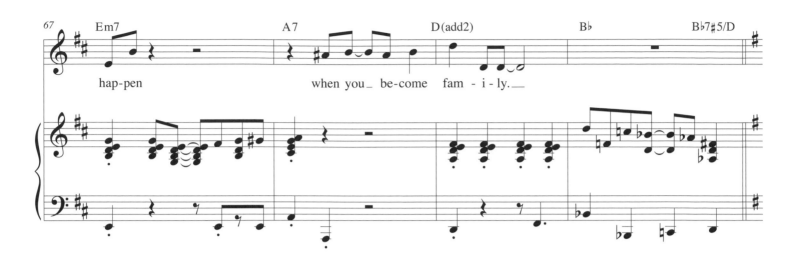

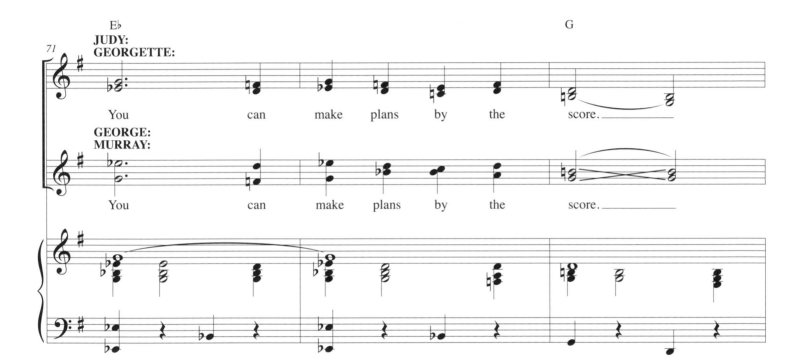

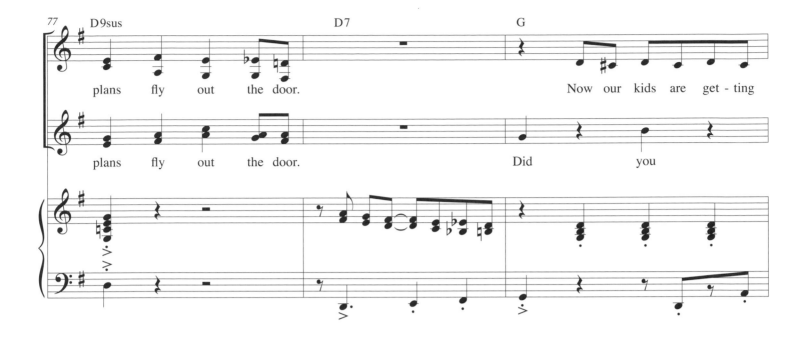